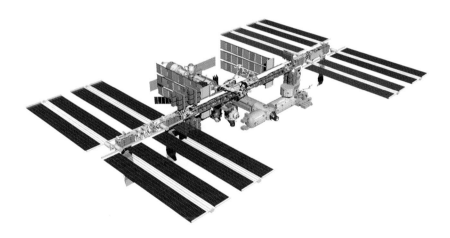

Published in 2014 by The Rosen Publishing Group, Inc.
29 East 21st Street, New York, NY 10010

Photo Credits: **KEY** tl=top left; tc=top center; tr=top right; cl=center left; c=center; cr=center right; bl=bottom left; bc=bottom center; br=bottom right; bg=background

CBT = Corbis; DT = Dreamstime; iS = istockphoto.com; N = NASA; SH = Shutterstock; SPL = Science Photo Library; TF = Topfoto; TPL = photolibrary.com

1c N; **7**bl, br iS; **9**bc TPL; **10**bc CBT; br SH; **12**cl SPL; bc, cr TF; **12–13**tc TPL; **13**cl CBT; cr DT; **14**bl iS; **16**bl, br, cr, tr iS; **17**cl, tl iS; **18**cl, tr iS; **18–19**bc iS; **19**tc iS; **22**cl TF; **26**c, cr N; **27**cl, cr, tc N; **28**bc N; **30**cr TF; **32**bg iS

All illustrations copyright Weldon Owen Pty Ltd. **10**tl, cl, bl Francesca D'Ottavi/Wilkinson Studios

WELDON OWEN PTY LTD
Managing Director: Kay Scarlett
Creative Director: Sue Burk
Publisher: Helen Bateman
Senior Vice President, International Sales: Stuart Laurence
Vice President Sales North America: Ellen Towell
Administration Manager, International Sales: Kristine Ravn

Publisher Cataloging Data

Coupe, Robert.
Wheels, wings, and motors / by Robert Coupe.
p. cm. — (Discovery education: how it works)
Includes index.
ISBN 978-1-4777-6313-1 (library binding) — ISBN 978-1-4777-6314-8 (pbk.) —
ISBN 978-1-4777-6315-5 (6-pack)
1. Transportation — Juvenile literature. I. Coupe, Robert. II. Title.
HE152.C68 2014
388—d23

Manufactured in the United States of America

CPSIA Compliance Information: Batch #W14PK2: For Further Information contact Rosen Publishing, New York, New York at 1-800-237-9932

WHEELS, WINGS, AND MOTORS

ROBERT COUPE

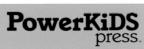

PowerKiDS press™

New York

Contents

Wheels, Wheels, Wheels..........................6

From Carriages to Cars 8

Bicycles..10

Wheels on Rails 12

Trains Today and Tomorrow...............14

From Sail to Steam 16

Boats and Ships Today........................18

First to Fly...20

Pioneers of Flight 22

Long-Distance Flight 24

Leaving Earth 26

Into Space and Back............................28

Mix and Match 30

Glossary...31

Index 32

Websites..32

Wheels, Wheels, Wheels

We rely on wheels for transportation, for making electricity, and for many other purposes. They are a necessary part of most machines, even fairly simple ones, such as can openers, that we use in our homes. People probably started using wheels more than 5,000 years ago. By about 4,000 years ago, chariots in Turkey had the first wheels with spokes in them.

Ancient times
People used logs to roll heavy loads from one place to another.

Ancient Sumer
Wood was clamped together and carved into a circle.

Ancient Rome
Wheels were lighter and wider and had spokes in them.

About 4000 BC
People rolled heavy stones for building on trunks of cut-down trees.

About 1000 BC
Ancient Egyptians had chariots with light wooden wheels and spokes.

About 300 BC
Ancient Romans built roads and used wagons to transport goods from place to place.

Early train wheels
These were made of solid iron and were linked together.

Bicycle wheels
Air-filled tires were used for the first time on bicycles.

Motorcycle wheels
These have rubber tires with tread. This provides friction, so the tires do not slip easily on the road.

AD 1800s
Steam trains carried passengers and goods over long distances at greater speeds than ever before.

About 1870
Early bicycles gave a very bumpy ride. Bicycles, like this penny-farthing, had solid rubber tires.

Modern times
Today, we depend more and more on fast-moving cars, trucks, and other road vehicles.

From Carriages to Cars

For thousands of years, people have used horses and other animals to pull chariots, carts, and wagons of different kinds. But it was not until 1886 that the first modern motor car, powered by a gasoline engine, was built. About 20 years later, many people in richer countries could afford to own and drive their own cars. Now, more than 40 million new cars are built every year.

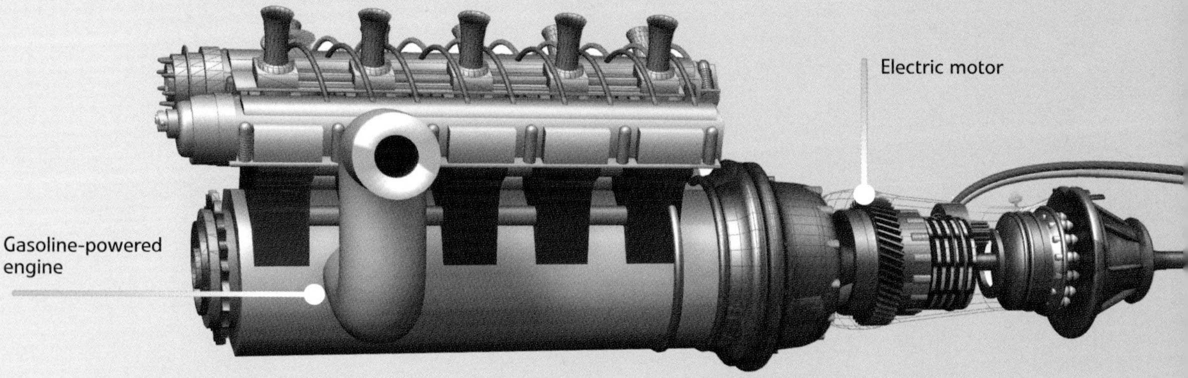

Electric motor

Gasoline-powered engine

About 1000 BC
Ancient Egyptians rode into battle on horse-drawn chariots with wooden wheels.

1769
Nicolas-Joseph Cugnot invented a steam-powered vehicle in France. It could move only very slowly.

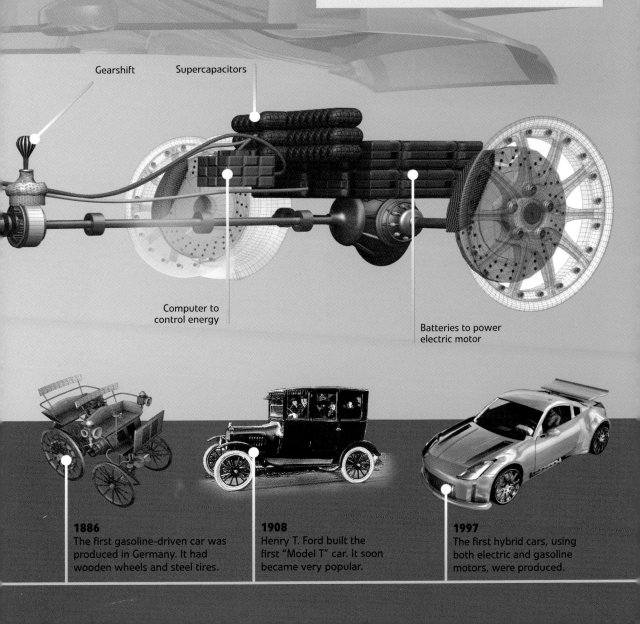

Hybrid cars

Fumes from gasoline engines pollute the atmosphere. Hybrid cars have a small gasoline motor, but also a clean electric motor that powers the car whenever possible. These cars are much cleaner than those that run on just gasoline.

Gearshift

Supercapacitors

Computer to control energy

Batteries to power electric motor

1886
The first gasoline-driven car was produced in Germany. It had wooden wheels and steel tires.

1908
Henry T. Ford built the first "Model T" car. It soon became very popular.

1997
The first hybrid cars, using both electric and gasoline motors, were produced.

Early bicycles
The first bicycles had either wooden or solid rubber tires. It was not until 1887 that John Dunlop invented the air-filled tires we use today. He invented them for his son's bike.

Dandy horse, 1790
The rider of this bike had to move it forward by pushing along the ground with his feet.

Penny-farthing, 1870
The rider sat over the large front wheel and used pedals to push the bike forward.

Safety bike, 1879
This was the first bike to have pedals attached to a chain that drove the back wheel.

Bicycles

The modern bicycle, or bike, was invented a little more than 130 years ago. Before that, bikes were difficult to ride, slow-moving, and often not very safe. Today, the bicycle is the main kind of transportation for many people throughout the world. It is also widely used for recreation and in races.

MOTORCYCLES

The first motorcycle powered by a gasoline engine was built in Germany in 1885. Nine years later, also in Germany, brothers Wilhelm and Heinrich Hildebrand and Alois Wolfmüller built the first motorcycles with air-filled rubber tires. Motorcycles are widely used for transportation and for racing.

Choppers
Motorcycles called choppers often have large front wheels and low, wide back wheels.

Harley-Davidson
This American company has been building motorcycles for more than 100 years. This one is from 1926.

Tour de France

This famous road race covers more than 1,860 miles (3,000 km) in France and is held over three weeks every year. It tests the strength and skill of all the cyclists who ride in it.

Wheels on Rails

Most trains now run on metal wheels that are pulled or driven along metal tracks. The first trains that are anything like today's ones were built during the first half of the 1800s. They had a steam-powered engine that pulled a number of carriages or trucks. Carriages carried passengers, and trucks were filled with coal or other goods. The engines were called locomotives. At the front of the locomotive, water was heated to boiling point by a coal fire. The steam produced by the boiling water drove the metal wheels that pulled the train along the parallel metal rails of the track.

1804
The first locomotive had a steam engine that pulled a mining truck behind it.

1829
George Stephenson's "Rocket" became the model for later locomotives.

1874
By this time, locomotives were more powerful and could pull heavier loads much faster.

CABLE CARS

Since the 1870s, visitors to San Francisco have enjoyed riding up and down the city's steep hills in four-wheeled tramcars pulled by cables set in the road between the rails. A driver, known as a gripman, uses a lever to hold and release the cable and to control the speed and movement of the car.

The *Orient Express*
This famous train transported passengers between Paris, France, and Istanbul, Turkey, for more than 80 years, until 1977.

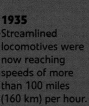

1935
Streamlined locomotives were now reaching speeds of more than 100 miles (160 km) per hour.

1940s
Diesel engines were combined with electric motors to produce even more power.

Today
Huge diesel-powered trains carry material from mines over great distances.

Trains Today and Tomorrow

Electric trains are now common in most parts of the world. The train's engine gets its power from overhead electric lines or from a track underneath. Some trains, called monorails, run on a single, wide track. The sides of the cars fold over the track, and wheels with rubber tires move along the bottom edges of the track. Electric motors drive these trains. In some places, monorails carry passengers high above the streets of large cities. The most modern trains of all do not run on wheels. They are called maglev (magnetic levitation) trains.

Future train
This is a design for a maglev train that may one day carry passengers underground at great speed between cities in Switzerland and France.

That's Amazing!

A maglev train in Shanghai, China, runs between the airport and the city at a top speed of 268 miles (431 km) per hour.

Monorail
A monorail in Sydney, Australia, opened in 1988. It carries passengers over parts of the city at an average speed of 20 miles (32 km) per hour.

NO WHEELS

A maglev train floats above a track below it as it speeds along. There are powerful magnets underneath the train's cars and at each side of the single, wide rail. These magnets combine to lift the train up and drive it along at high speed.

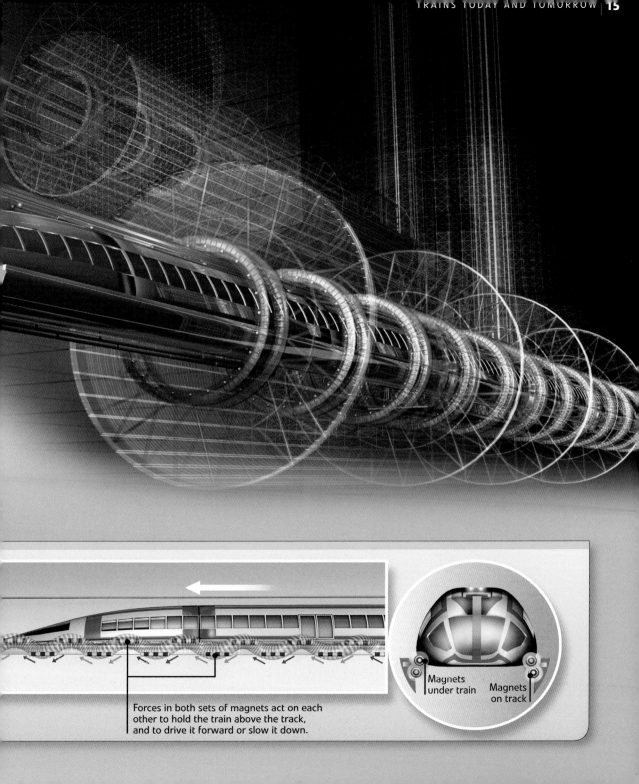

Forces in both sets of magnets act on each other to hold the train above the track, and to drive it forward or slow it down.

Magnets under train

Magnets on track

From Sail to Steam

Boats were invented long before the wheel. More than 40,000 years ago, people in canoes paddled across shallow seas. About 5,000 years ago, Egyptians developed the first sailing boats. Around 2,000 years ago, Chinese sailors invented the rudder. This made steering much easier. Over many centuries, people gradually developed bigger, faster, and safer sailing ships that could travel great distances around the world. During the 1800s, large steamships began to move people and goods more quickly and comfortably around the world's oceans.

About 1000 BC
Sailors traveled across the Pacific Ocean in canoes powered by oars and sails.

Early 1400s
Huge Chinese junks sailed from China to India, Southeast Asia, Africa, and the Middle East.

About 3500 BC
Egyptian trading boats traveled along the Nile River.

1492
The *Santa Maria*, the main ship in Christopher Columbus's fleet, sailed from Spain to America.

Mid–1800s
Clippers were large sailing boats that had enormous canvas sails driving them forward.

Early 1900s
Large ocean liners, driven by powerful steam turbine engines, carried passengers across the Atlantic Ocean.

Boats and Ships Today

Most modern ships are driven by huge engines that turn large propellers at the back of the ship, below the water. In earlier days, ships' engines were powered by steam. Now they use diesel fuel. The propellers spin rapidly to push the ship forward in the water. Also at the back of the ship, near the propellers, is a rudder. The rudder steers the ship. When it is angled sideways in one direction, it causes the ship to turn in the opposite direction.

Oil tanker
An oil tanker carries oil that will be made into gasoline and other products. The oil is stored in large tanks below the deck and inside the hull.

Luxury cruise ship
Most people now make long journeys by plane. But luxury liners still take people on long vacations at sea.

Container ship
Stacked up on the deck of this ship are containers that carry
many types of goods between countries around the world.

Private boats
Some people can afford to own
their own yachts or motor-powered
cruisers. They use them to take
themselves and their friends on
cruising holidays or day outings.

First to Fly

Throughout the ages, people everywhere have dreamed of flying. There are many ancient legends about people and gods that could fly. One ancient Greek myth tells of Pegasus, a flying horse. But it was not until 1783 that people flew for the first time. On October 19 of that year, in Paris, France, a hot air balloon, built by brothers Étienne and Joseph Montgolfier, carried two men up into the air and safely back to the ground. A large crowd of amazed people gathered to watch this historic event.

Did You Know?

A month before the first human flight, a duck, rooster, and sheep became the first-ever passengers to fly in a Montgolfier hot air balloon. The flight lasted eight minutes.

Rope to hold down balloon

Wooden post

Fire power

Hot air is lighter than cold air, so when the air inside the Montgolfier brothers' balloon was heated by a fire underneath, it lifted off the ground. As the air inside slowly cooled down, the balloon and its passengers drifted slowly downward.

Fire to heat air

Balloon made
of silk and paper

HEATING AND COOLING

Modern hot air balloons have a gas burner,
which the pilot turns up and down to provide
more or less heat. That lets the pilot control
the height at which the balloon will fly.
To move downward, the pilot pulls a ripcord.
This opens a vent at the top of the balloon
that lets hot air escape.

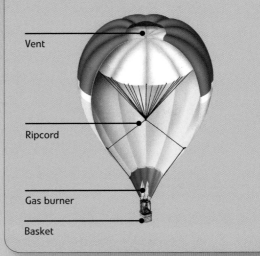

Vent

Ripcord

Gas burner

Basket

Early designs
The Italian artist and inventor
Leonardo da Vinci sketched ideas
for a flying machine based on bird
wings. It was called an ornithopter.

Pioneers of Flight

I n the late 1800s, inventors competed with each other to build a flying machine that was heavier than air. Some weird and wonderful machines were built. Many of them had heavy steam-driven engines. None of these managed to fly. A very early, successful, heavier-than-air flight was in 1853, in a glider built by Sir George Cayley. Gliders do not have engines. They glide through the air on air currents. It was not until 1903 that Orville Wright made the first-ever flight in an engine-driven aircraft.

Wright brothers
Wilbur and Orville Wright built the first successful aircraft in 1903. It was powered by a gasoline engine that drove a single large propeller.

Steam engine
In 1894 in England, Sir Hiram Maxim built a steam-driven plane. It failed to get off the ground.

Early glider flight
In 1853, Sir George Cayley's glider flew a distance of 900 feet (275 m). The pilot was one of Cayley's servants.

Across the Atlantic Ocean
In 1927, Charles Lindbergh made the first solo flight across the Atlantic Ocean, from New York to Paris. His plane was named *Spirit of St. Louis*.

First jet
In 1939, the first jet aircraft, the Heinkel He 178, took off from an airfield in Germany. Air was drawn in through the nose of the plane, and hot gases exploded from the rear end.

Long-Distance Flight

The flight pioneers of the 1800s and early 1900s could never have imagined the aircraft that fly millions of people around the world today. One of the first passenger aircraft was the Handley Page W8. This was a biplane with an upper wing directly above the two lower wings. It carried up to 15 passengers on trips between London, England, and places in Europe. It flew at about 85 miles (137 km) per hour. Its pilot and copilot sat in an uncovered cockpit at the front. Some modern airliners can carry more than 800 people at speeds of 560 miles (900 km) per hour.

De Havilland DH 106 Comet
This was the first jet-powered passenger aircraft. It carried 44 people.

Lockheed L-188 Electra
This plane began operating in 1957. It carried more than 100 passengers.

That's Amazing!
Concorde cruised at 1,320 miles (2,125 km) per hour—faster than the speed of sound. It took just three and a half hours to travel from New York to Paris.

Boeing 747
Arriving in the 1970s, the "jumbo jet" has been the iconic long-distance aircraft for more than 30 years.

Douglas DC-3

This was introduced in 1935. It carried up to 21 passengers in safety and comfort. It was the first truly modern passenger aircraft to operate.

Airbus A380

This is the largest passenger aircraft ever built. It can carry up to 800 people on two decks.

CONCORDE

Introduced in 1969, Concorde was the fastest ever passenger aircraft. It flew between New York, Paris, and London. The nose of Concorde moved up and down. This helped with landing and taking off. A Concorde crashed near Paris in 2001. Concordes stopped flying in 2003.

Nose up for flying

Nose down for landing

Nose lower down for takeoff

Leaving Earth

For hundreds of years, people have been using telescopes to learn about the planets and stars in the universe. But it was only a little more than 50 years ago that scientists sent the first satellite, *Sputnik 1*, out into space to travel in orbit around our planet. Four years later, a Russian astronaut became the first person to travel into space. He circled Earth for 108 minutes. Since then, American astronauts have been to the Moon six times and many other astronauts have traveled into space. Unmanned machines, called probes, have visited other planets and sent back a large amount of information about them.

That's Amazing!
The first traveler in space was not a human. In 1957, a Russian dog, called Laika, went up into space in a satellite.

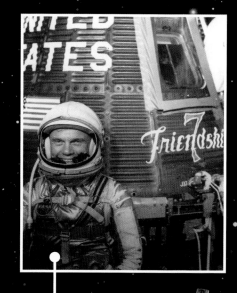

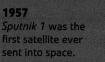

1957
Sputnik 1 was the first satellite ever sent into space.

1961
The first person to travel to space was Yuri Gagarin.

1962
The first American to orbit Earth was John Glenn.

1962
The US *Mariner 2* was the first probe to reach another planet, Venus.

INTERNATIONAL SPACE STATION

The International Space Station (ISS) is a huge building in space. It is as big as a football field, and it flies in orbit around Earth. Seven astronauts can live, work, and carry out experiments there for long periods. It has taken more than 11 years to build.

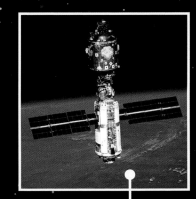

1969
Humans landed on the Moon for the first time.

1976
Viking 1 was the first space probe to land on Mars.

1989
The first space probe to Neptune was *Voyager 2*.

1998
The first part of the ISS was launched.

Into Space and Back

American astronauts went to the Moon six times between 1969 and 1972. They went there in a number of spacecraft called Apollo. The astronauts traveled in the front part of the spacecraft, known as the Command Module. During the journey, rockets that powered the craft fell away. By the time the astronauts returned to Earth, only the Command Module remained. This splashed down into the ocean, and could not be used again. In 1981, the US launched a kind of spacecraft that could go into space many times. When it came back to Earth, it landed on a runway, just like an airplane. This was the first space shuttle.

Flight deck
The commander and pilot controlled the shuttle from here.

Thermal tiles
These protected against extreme heat as the shuttle flew back into Earth's atmosphere.

On the Moon
Astronauts landed on the Moon in a part of the Apollo spacecraft called the Lunar Module. This is the taller machine in the background.

Robotic arm
This moved satellites and other equipment in and out of the payload bay.

Astronauts
Astronauts in space suits worked outside the shuttle to repair a satellite.

Main engines
The three main engines got their fuel from a tank outside the space shuttle. This tank fell away when the shuttle went into orbit around Earth.

Payload bay
Satellites and other equipment were carried in this part of the shuttle.

Orbital engines
Two engines in the tail controlled the shuttle when it was orbiting Earth.

Doors
Doors along the back opened to allow equipment to be moved in and out.

Space shuttle

Astronauts in space shuttles took new satellites into space. They also repaired satellites already in orbit and carried out scientific experiments. Shuttles also carried astronauts and supplies to the International Space Station.

There are plans in the US to build a new spacecraft that will travel farther out in space, as far as the planet Mars.

Mix and Match

Can you find the word on the right that matches each description on the left?

A

1 These help drive ships and aircraft

2 The power that drove ships and trains during the 1800s

3 Brothers who made the first hot air balloon

4 Ancient people who were the first to use rudders on boats

5 A type of train that floats above a track underneath it

6 Spacecraft that traveled to the Moon

7 A passenger aircraft that flew faster than the speed of sound

8 A bicycle with one very large and one much smaller wheel

B

maglev

penny-farthing

Chinese

Apollo

Concorde

propellers

steam

Montgolfier

Glossary

astronauts (AS-truh-nots)
People who travel or work
in space.

biplane (BY-playn)
An older type of aircraft that
had an upper wing directly
above the lower wings.

computer (kum-PYOO-tur)
A machine that automatically
performs tasks, such as
making calculations or
controlling how other
machines work.

diesel (DEE-zel)
A heavy oil that is used as
fuel for some motor vehicles,
ships, and trains.

gasoline (GA-suh-leen)
A liquid made from oil that
burns easily and is used as
fuel for many motor vehicles,
aircraft, and other machines.

hybrid (HY-brud)
A mixture of two different
kinds of things. A hybrid
car has two different kinds
of motors.

iconic (eye-KO-nik)
Describes a symbolic
representation
of something.

junk (JUNK)
A type of sailing ship with
a flat bottom that is used in
China and other parts of Asia.

liner (LY-nur)
A very large ship that takes
passengers on long sea
journeys.

Lunar Module
(LOO-nur MAH-jool)
A machine in which
astronauts traveled from
their spacecraft to the
surface of the Moon.

maglev (MAG-lev)
A train that floats above a
single track as it moves
along. "Maglev" is short for
magnetic levitation.

monorail (MAH-noh-rayl)
A kind of train that travels
on only one rail.

probes (PROHBZ)
Machines that travel into
space, often to other planets.
They send scientific
information back to Earth.

propeller (pruh-PEL-ur)
A set of blades that spin
rapidly to push a ship
through the water or an
aircraft through the air.

rockets (RAH-kets)
Vehicles driven by burning
gases that are forced
out at the back, which
force the rocket forward
or upward.

satellites (SA-tih-lyts)
Machines in space that travel
around Earth or other planets
and send information back
to Earth.

spokes (SPOHKS)
Rods or bars that connect
the outer edge of a wheel
to the center of the wheel.

turbine (TUR-byn)
A wheel with blades that
a gas, such as steam, or
a liquid, such as water,
forces to turn at great
speed. Turbines are
used to drive machines or
to make electricity.

Index

A

aircraft 20, 21, 22, 23, 24,
    25, 28, 30
Apollo 28

B

bicycles 7, 10, 11

C

cable cars 13
cars 7, 8, 9
choppers 10
computers 9
Concorde 24, 25

D

diesel 13, 18
Dunlop, John 10

E

Egyptians 6, 8, 16
electricity 6, 9, 14

F

Ford, Henry T. 9

G

Gagarin, Yuri 26
gasoline 8, 9, 10, 18, 22
Glenn, John 26
gliders 22

H

Harley-Davidson 10
Hildebrand brothers 11
hot air balloons 20, 21
hybrid cars 9

I

International Space Station
    (ISS) 27, 29

J

jet aircraft 23, 24, 25

M

maglev trains 14, 15
Model T cars 9
monorail 14
Montgolfier brothers 20
motorcycles 7, 10

P

penny-farthing bicycles 7, 10

R

Romans 6

S

satellites 26, 29
ships 16, 17, 18, 19, 30
spacecraft 26, 27, 28, 29
space probes 26, 27
Spirit of St. Louis 23
steam 7, 8, 12, 16, 17,
    18, 22
Stephenson, George 12
Sumer 6

T

tires 7, 9, 10, 14
Tour de France 11
trains 7, 12, 13, 14, 15, 30

W

wheels 6, 7
Wright brothers 22

Websites

Due to the changing nature of Internet links, PowerKids Press has developed an online list of websites related to the subject of this book. This site is updated regularly. Please use this link to access the list:
www.powerkidslinks.com/disc/wheel/